Sympathetic Magic Of The Ainu - The Native People Of Japan

By

John Batchelor

Sympathetic Magic.

General remarks—Objection to being photographed—*Ichashkara*, 'enclosing a person within a fence'—Trees used in magic—Rain-making — Producing bad weather — Producing fine weather.

SYMPATHETIC magic is one of the most extraordinary cults there is, and can be far more easily illustrated by example than explained by exact definition. It is so closely connected with disease, fetishism, and totemism, in many respects, that it appears to me that any person who makes a study of the subject must find it really very difficult to tell with anything like precision where one ends and the other begins. Lubbock, in his *Origin of Civilisation*, says, 'The king of the Koussa Kaffirs having broken off a piece of a stranded anchor died soon after, upon which all the Kaffirs looked upon the anchor as alive, and saluted it respectfully whenever they passed near it.' The *Tusu guru*, that is, Ainu wizards, men and women, of three widely-separated villages, told the people that the late great floods in Yezo (1898) were owing to the presence of myself as a teacher of Christianity, and were sent as a punishment to the Ainu for some of them having adopted the Christian religion. Epidemic diseases

Objection to being Photographed.

too have been set down to a like cause. All these are forms of sympathetic magic, and the illustrations are given in order to show the kind of thing this and the next chapter are intended to explain.

One of the most exaggerated expressions of thought connected with this cult is, perhaps, to be found in the matter of the photograph or sketch, though, in so far as the Ainu are concerned, this is not so much the case now as formerly. On this matter I wrote in the *Journal of the American Folk-Lore Society* as follows:—

'AINU OBJECTION TO BEING PHOTOGRAPHED.

'It was an old belief among the Ainu—a belief which has now almost entirely died out in Yezo—that by being sketched or photographed, especially when in naked condition, their natural life is thereby shortened in some mysterious way or other. The term the people use with reference to this is, *Ainu katu ehange*, "the man draws nigh to his form;" and that is like saying, "death is at hand," or "the man is becoming a ghost." Even so late as the year 1890 a gentleman travelling in Yezo had his sketch-block taken away by the Ainu, because he was sketching them when they were nearly naked. The people appeared to see something uncanny in having their mere form produced without the substance. To speak of the form of a person is often equivalent to speaking of his soul, spirit, or ghost. Hence to produce a person's form on paper was considered to be like drawing the soul out of him and placing it in an unnatural position, and the man himself was henceforth supposed to be gradually shadowing off into mere psychical form without material substance. In short, the Ainu appeared to think that by having his photograph taken a person was thereby transformed into a ghost before his time.'

The person I have just referred to is not the only one who has inadvertently got into trouble in this way. Mr. B. Douglas Howard, who travelled in Saghalien for a short time, has given us his experiences among the Ainu who dwell there. In his book, which is entitled *Trans-Siberian Savages*, I find two passages which illustrate the point under discussion, though he does not appear to be aware of the reasons for the Ainu aversion to the camera. I now quote from that book the two passages referred to. On page 95 we find that Mr. Howard brought out his hand mirror for the inspection of the people. He says: 'This, to my astonishment, quickly produced exactly the effect my rifle failed to accomplish. As fast as I showed them their faces, they darted like arrows through the doorway, and nothing could induce them to come back. I do not wonder at it,' etc. Evidently Mr. Howard thought that it was their own filth or ugliness they were afraid of. But he should have looked deeper than that, for it would be unnatural for them to consider themselves, brought up as they are, either dirty or ugly, whatever Mr. Howard may have thought of them. The fact, however, is explained by the Ainu words, *Ainu katu ehange*,

AN AINU BEAR HUNTER
(*Dressed in one of the author's cast-off suits*).

'the man draws nigh to his form.'

Mr. Howard says :—

'In a very quiet way I have taken a good many carefully selected snapshots with my camera, which included the old chief, the wizard, and several other portraits. Thinking I would like to add to their pleasure another entirely new surprise and sensation, and also, perhaps, to impress them still further with my own wonderful powers, I took an almost endless amount of trouble to develope a few of them, especially the portraits. Of these, the only one now in my possession is a portrait of the old chief.

'The worst part of it is, that my loss of the others is due to a calamity which such immense pains innocently brought about.

'One day, when several men were in the hut with the chief, I took the opportunity to attempt a surprise, and watched the effect upon them as I displayed before them their newly-finished portraits. Instantly they sprang to their feet as if they had been shot. All except the chief rushed out of the hut as if in a rage. The old chief stamped up and down the hut in the greatest distress. Hearing a great hubbub, mixed with wild cries outside, I went to the hut door, where I found these people, whose gentle virtues I had so faithfully depicted, raving and gesticulating in the most menacing manner. To my utter consternation, I saw that some of them were brandishing sticks, some of them knives—that, indeed, one and all were suddenly changed to savages of the wildest type.

'Utterly bewildered at the sudden change of

Exercising Magic.

affairs, yet assuming that the pictures must have in some way been the cause of it, and remembering as I did the effect of the looking-glass upon them, I appealed as well as I could to the chief, exhibited my regret, and tried to make him understand that I placed myself and everything I had in his hands. To make a clean breast of it, I brought out my pictures, my apparatus, and everything that pertained to it, and offered to put them all into the fireplace; but there was no fire. Meanwhile, the people outside grew so violent that the chief was obliged to go out to them.

'After a long parley, the chief returned and made me understand that I must carry everything outside. As fast as they could do it a big fire was kindled in front of the hut. *Inaos* were stuck in the ground all around the fire, and following their intimations, while they stood back in great alarm, I threw my poor kodak, my pictures, all my apparatus, on the fire, and stood there calmly looking on till nothing was left of them but ashes.'

The Ainu name for the cult we know as sympathetic magic is *ichashkara, i.e.* 'enclosing in a fence,' and there are several ways of exercising this black art. As retailed to me some of them are as follows:—

'Should a man or woman have a quarrel, and desire to compass their enemies' hurt by magic, he or she should procure some mugwort, and make an image to represent his enemy's body. This image is called *imosh*. When made, a hole should be dug in the ground not far from the house, and the image cursed and placed in it upside down.

The prayer to be used at such times is as follows :—

'"O demon who art called *toipuk-un-chiri*, *i.e.* under-ground-bird-demon,' I give this image of the person I hate to thee: take his soul and carry it together with his body to hell: oh turn thou mine enemy into one of thy own kind, make a devil of him."

'If this be done, the person who has been cursed will fall sick and die. His body will rot away as the image decomposes.'

'Another way of avenging oneself on an enemy is to place the image beneath the trunk of a rotten tree. After being thus buried the following prayer should be said :—" O demon, make the body of the man represented by this image to rot with this tree, and let his life gradually fade away with it. O thou demon named *toikunrari tumunchi* —hear me, and quickly take his soul, and turn it into one of thy own kind." If this prayer be said with earnestness, the Ainu will soon die—yea, his body will rot with the tree and he will perish from off the earth.'

Another method employed is to take a piece of *yarape-ni*, *i.e.* 'the gueldre rose,' make it into an *inao*, and ask it to carry the soul of the enemy to hell. After this the *inao* is taken and buried upside down.

Another way told me is as follows :—

'Should a person wish to bring evil upon another by means of sympathetic magic, he should make a boat of rotten wood. When this is done he should make images of two men, also of rotten

Sympathetic Magic.

wood, and place them on board. He should then say the following prayer: "O ye demons, I have made the images of two men, one of which represents my enemy. Pray take his soul and thrust it into hell. Take it right away to *Uchiura moshiri*, yea, carry it off to that place." Should he do this, the man will quickly die.'

My informant also told me that there are some very bad women who bewitch their husbands. Thus, for example, should a woman desire to get rid of her spouse by death, she may kill him in the following way. 'She should take his head-dress, wrap it up in a bag in the shape of a corpse ready prepared for burial, dig a deep hole and place it in it. She should then pray, saying: "When this head-dress and bag rot, may my husband also die and rot with them. It is for this I am now digging his grave. O thou demon named *Toiko-shimpuk*, hear me. Be quick and take the soul of this man, and make it into one of thine own kind." If this prayer be said, her husband will die in a very short time.'

Trees, too, of some kinds, are also used for the purpose of executing vengeance on one's personal enemies. Such, for example, are the gueldre rose, elder, poplar, elm, and some others. These trees are called *wen chikuni*, *i.e.* 'evil trees,' because they are used for evil purposes, and are supposed to be full of demons. When any of them are required to act against one's enemies they are worshipped, for they are supposed to have life: and the Ainu is nothing if not animistic in his religious and superstitious belief. When prayed to the form of prayer is:—

'O thou tree: O thou demon called *Nishinnai-samnioyashi tu'n unchi*,'—*i.e.* 'devil by the waste places, where the trees stand'—'I worship thee and make a request unto thee. Listen now to what I have to say. There are many men persecuting me, and I make known to thee their names. Do thou hasten and take away their souls: oh make them demons like unto thyself.'

If this prayer be said, evil will surely overtake one's foes.

Some of the *inao*—explained in chapters nine to twelve—may be taken as a means by which to exercise sympathetic magic; the same may also be said of the use of hares' paws (to be spoken of later on), and the fact, too, that snakes are invited to bite one's enemies (also to be spoken of later on) may be found to have their first principles in this cult.

That the powers of the air can be influenced by the actions of men by way of sympathetic magic is apparent from the following incident. On the occasion of some very dry weather, when the land was parched and the gardens suffering from want of water, I heard the Ainu talking about 'rain-making,' during the discussion of which subject several new words and phrases struck upon my ear. One phrase was *shiriwen hokki marapto*, 'ceremony for producing wet weather;' and another was *shiriwen hokki guru*, 'the person who produces wet weather;' and another was *apto ashte guru*, 'the person who causes it to rain.'

Producing Rain.

When the Ainu desire to perform the ceremony of 'rain-making,' the people are collected together, and prayer is said to the goddess of fire, rivers, and springs by the appointed 'rain-maker.' Abundant libations of wine are, of course, offered and drunk. The master of the ceremonies then appoints certain men to head small companies, and command them to proceed to execute particular functions. One man is told to take his company to the river's brink, and there to see that each one washes his tobacco box and pipe in the running water. Another is ordered to catch a small fish, called *eshokka*, light a pipe, and take the stem and place it in its mouth; the fish thereupon closes its mouth, and in the act draws in a little of the smoke, which is seen to escape from the gills. After this the fish is allowed to escape. Another party is commanded to take a porringer, fit it up with sails, and place oars in it as though it were a boat. Next, some are told to push and others to draw it about the village and gardens. Another party is told to take sieves and scatter water about with them. Both men and women are allowed to take part in these proceedings. The Ainu say that if the ceremony is properly conducted rain is sure to follow. A short time ago I saw some Ainu who were longing for rain dress up a dog in a most fantastic fashion, and amid much noise and laughter lead it about the garden; this was to make rain. We had a heavy downfall that very night, and so the ceremony was proved successful; consequently the Ainu have stronger faith than ever in their ability to produce rain, for the powers of the air were thereby proved to take notice of the actions of men.

Another curious way of making rain was told me as follows. 'The animals that act as cooks, *i.e.*, racoons, are very fiery-tempered and quickly hear when addressed, and so it comes to pass that when a person sacrifices one he presents *inao* to its head and prays to it. Again, when men go to the fisheries they take the skulls of the animals with them. The reason is that when the weather is continuously calm, and the men have to work incessantly both by day and by night, they get tired and long for a rest. At such calms they take out their racoon skulls at night and pray to them. The prayer used is: "This calm is lasting too long; we are very tired; please send us bad weather, so that we may not be able to work." After this prayer has been said they throw water over one another and make merry. If this be done properly, bad storms are certain to follow, and then the people get rest and are greatly rejoiced. As soon as the rough weather begins the men buy *saké*, worship, and offer libations to the skull; if very bad weather indeed is required, the people make gloves and caps of racoon and marten skins, put them on and dance. This procures very great storms.'

But not only do the people imagine they can produce bad weather at will, but fine also. Thus, on a very cold day (namely Nov. 24, 1900) I went into a hut, and found some convolvulus roots spitted and placed near the fire upon the hearth. Upon asking the reason of this I

Sympathetic Magic.

found that it was to bring fine, warm weather, because the master of the hut and I had been out that day on a somewhat long ride. No doubt the intention was good, but I cannot say that I felt any warmer for it.

Sympathetic Magic-

The water-ousel—The flying squirrel—Bewitching by cutting one's clothes—Divination by fox's skull.

THE last chapter was devoted to certain methods by which it was supposed one can injure another by sympathetic magic. There are other matters connected with this subject which may not be passed over, and they are the supposed effect of one living being upon another, and direct witchcraft. As regards the former matter, I will take a bird and an animal acting upon a man, and with reference to the latter a case of witchcraft by cutting one's clothes will be given.

I was one day out with an Ainu trying to shoot something for our larder, and on our way brought down a water-ousel. The Ainu begged me to give him its heart. I asked him why, and he then explained that if he took out the heart and ate it raw and while warm, he would be able to stand fatigue, would wax eloquent, and would be able to shoot as well and quickly as I did on that occasion. I granted his request and he ate the heart; but I find that he gets tired just as soon as he used, shoots no straighter and is no more eloquent than he was before, though he himself thinks he has

The Water-Ousel.

improved in all these respects. Why the spirit of the water-ousel has this particular power to act on the soul of man rather than that of any other bird I was unable to find out. All this man could tell me was that the fact had been taught him by his forefathers, and I certainly find the same idea universal among the Ainu, though the kind of birds vary, the heart of one bird being considered good for this purpose and the heart of another good for that.

On talking to another Ainu acquaintance on this point, he supplied me with the following legend connected with this bird and custom :—

THE LEGEND OF THE WATER-OUSEL.

'The water-ousel came down from heaven. He is of a black colour, and lives along the watercourses. His heart is exceedingly wise, and in speech he is most eloquent. When therefore he is killed he should be immediately torn open, and his heart wrenched out and swallowed. This should be done before it gets cold or damaged in any way. If a man swallows it at once, he will become very fluent and wise, and will also be able to overcome all his opponents in argument. But the water-ousel has power to help in another way. For not only does he make people eloquent, but he also makes all who swallow his heart prosper in wealth far above their neighbours. The person who is fortunate enough to swallow one is called by the special name of *Chikoshinninup epirika guru, i.e.* 'the person who has gained a charm.' For this reason the water-ousel is to be worshipped and has *inao* offered to him.'

There appears to be something akin to this in the treatment of the eyes of animals taken in hunting. In Dobell's *Travels in Siberia*, vol. i., page 19, we read that 'when the Kamtchadales kill a bear they stick a sharp knife into each eye and rip up the belly. This, they say, is quite necessary, as bears have sometimes been known to recover, even after severe wounds, and kill the persons who have ripped them up, with the intention of skinning them. Whereas, they say, if their eyes had first been put out they would not have seen anything, and those persons would have escaped.'

The Ainu with whom I have had anything to do seem to know nothing of this custom. When a man kills a bear or a deer, he first skins it, cuts off the head, and then carefully takes out the eyes. Some hunters swallow the eyes raw, while others tenderly place them, especially those of bears, on a leaf with *inao* shavings, and put them outside the east end of the huts by the *nusa*. I have several times asked them why they are swallowed, and the only replies I have so far obtained are that they consider them too beautiful and precious to be thrown away, or else too sweet to the taste. But I have a suspicion that, whatever may be the reason now, they originally swallowed them either as fetiches, by way of sympathetic magic to render them clear-sighted when hunting and shooting, or as charms to prevent themselves from being bewitched by the animals they have killed.

The Flying Squirrel.

I find also that the flying squirrel holds a very high place in the cult practised among this people.

The Ainu place this animal among the birds, but this is because they fly; and we will not quarrel with them because they are a little out in some of their ornithological notions. In cases where there is lack of family issue, the men, after earnestly appealing to the goddess of fire and her consort for help, often place their hopes on the flying squirrel, though as a last resource they often marry a second or even a third wife. The name by which the flying squirrel is known is *At kamui*, and that is said to mean 'the divine prolific one.' It is so called because it is said to produce as many as thirty young at a birth. When partaken of, the flesh is supposed to convey power, in some unexplained way, to generate children. One might therefore very reasonably be led to imagine that childless women would be glad to get hold of one of them, to keep by her as a visible charm.

But, strange to say, such is not the case. This animal may not be stowed away and used as a charm, neither may it be worshipped after having been once sacrificed, and the feast in which its flesh is eaten been celebrated. The feast too has to be made in secret, and no one may be allowed to know of it save the husband —not even the woman herself. The legend about this matter is very curious, and I cannot do better, I think, than let it speak for itself to the reader, that he may draw his own conclusions.

Legend of the Flying Squirrel.

The Flying Squirrel was made by God and sent down to this world. The meaning of the name *At kamui* is "prolific one," and the reason for this name being given it is said to be as follows: This bird is exceedingly prolific, and the young it bears are very numerous indeed. One bird has been known sometimes to bear as many as thirty young at once. Therefore it is called *At kamui, i.e.* "the Divine prolific one." When a woman has no children, her husband should go to the mountain and hunt for one of these birds. Should he be successful in killing one, he should carry it home secretly. Upon arrival he should cut the flesh up into small pieces, boil it, and when cooked, carefully place it upon a tray. He should then offer *inao* to the head and skin, and pray thus: "O thou very prolific one, I have sacrificed thee for one reason only, and that is, that I may use thy flesh as a medicine for procuring children. Henceforth please cause my wife to bear me a child." After this prayer has been said he should take the meat, tell his wife that it is the flesh of some kind of bird (by no means letting her know that it is a flying squirrel), and give it her to eat. If this be properly done, the woman will be certain to bear some very fine children. This is the feast which is called *uatama marapto, i.e.* "the feast of placing the prolific one." If the woman, however, should know or even so much as guess that she was eating of this particular feast it would be quite useless, and

Witchcraft.

she would bear no children. For this reason the whole thing must be done in profound secrecy. When this bird has many children, it keeps them quiet by singing in a voice which sounds like *at ahun, at ahun*, "the prolific one enters, the prolific one enters." It must be carefully remembered that this bird may not be kept as a charm or fetich.'

No doubt the idea of witchcraft takes its root in sympathetic magic. This is very clearly illustrated in a case which happened under my own eye, the subject of which has been with me ever since it took place. The case shows how careful the people think one should be not to allow an enemy to get hold of any of his clothes, for should he do so he will cut them, and in that way destroy the life of the owner.

I sent an account of the case to the Asiatic Society of Japan, and the following few pages are a reproduction of the article.

The word under discussion is—

ISHIRISHINA (*to bewitch*).

'The Ainu being such a highly superstitious race as they have been proved to be, and such strong believers in the existence of very powerful spiritual beings both of a good and evil disposition, which are constantly making themselves felt among us and upon us through innumerable agencies, and seeing, moreover, that this people is unshaken in its belief that there is a great dualistic warfare ever raging in the world, and that the one object for which this battle is carried on is the good or ill, weal or woe of mankind, we are not at all surprised to find that they also believe in human witchcraft, and stand in great dread of the witch. A curious case of supposed witchcraft has just come under my notice, and the person thought to be bewitched is at the present moment (Feb. 17, 1896), under my roof at Sapporo. He is a man

THE AINU'S ACCOUNT.

Ku tashum wa ku hotke wa ku an, awa, orota Nupkipet un tusu-guru ek wa ku kot tashum aisamka kuni ne ari iki koro an. Koroka, kuani anak ne ku umbipka wa moshima no ku an. Awa, orowa ku mipihi hasami ani ayaspa wa an; koroka, heikachi hene iki ruwe ne kuni ku ramu gusu, moshima no ku an. Awa, tusu-guru ene itak-hi:—
'Nep gusu e mipihi ayaspa hike moshima no an ya?' sekoro itak. 'Nep gusu ne ya?' ari ku itak. Awa, ene itak-hi:—Kugoro 'yupo machihi amip yaspa ruwe ne,' sekoro itak. 'Tambe anak ne shi no wen kamui turen wa gusu iki-hi ne,' sekoro itak. Koroka, ku umbipka gusu, moshima no ku an. Awa, ku goro michi otta oman wa nei no ye nisa. Orota kugoro michi ene itak-hi:—'Son no e tusu wa e eramu ambe ne yakun, nei shiwentop turen wen kamui obosore kuni ne, Kamui otta ye, yakun, pirika, sekoro itak. Tambe gusu, nei tusu-guru Kamui otta inonno-itak; awa, nei shiwentep shi-kashke wa Nikap kotan ta koro yupo tak gusu

A Case of Bewitching.

aged 29, and has for a long time been suffering from a disease which has developed into *enteritis acuta*. Last autumn a medicine-man[*] came to his house, and informed him that he was bewitched by his elder brother's wife, and offered to cure him of the malady induced by the witch. But, in order that the whole case may be placed before you, I here give *in toto* what I wrote down from the man's lips when he told me of the matter, leaving explanations for the end.

TRANSLATION.

As I was lying ill a medicine-man came to me to perform ceremonies in order to do away with my complaint. But as I did not believe in him I left him to himself. Now, my clothes had been cut with a pair of scissors; but supposing it to have been done by a lad, I thought no more of it. Then the medicine-man said:— 'Why do you let this matter of cut clothes abide?' I replied, 'Ah, why is it?' He then told me that 'the wife of my elder brother had cut the clothes.' 'This,' he said, 'has happened through the influence of the very evil god (devil).' But as I did not believe him, I let the matter alone. Upon this he went to my father and said the same to him. My father replied, 'If by your divination you surely know this, it will be well for you to ask God to drive out the devil which acted through the woman.' Therefore the medicine-

---

[*] Wizard.

The Ainu's Account—*continued*.

oman wa tura wa ek hine, nei okkaiyo ene itak-hi:—'Son no shiwentep amip yaspa ruwe he an, tusu-guru otta ye wa inu,' sekoro itak. Kuani anak ne ku umbipka gusu ku uni ta ku hotke wa ku an; awa, orota nei shiwentep yupihi en hotuyekara wa ku oman; awa, nei guru ne yakka ene itak-hi:—'Eani moshima shiwentep e eramasui wa gusu shomo e mipihi ayaspa ruwe he an?' sekoro itak. Shi no ku irushka: 'Kuani anak ne tashum patek ku ki wa ku hotke wa ku an, awa, nep shiwentep ku eramasu hawe ne ya?' ari ku itak. 'Orowa, kuani anak ne pon heikachi hene iki ruwe ne kuni ku ramu gusu, moshima no ku an, awa, tan tusu-guru shiwentep iki ruwe ne sekoro itak; koroka, ku umbipka gusu moshima no ku an, awa, orota echi araki wa ene echi itakhi an. Kuani anak ne ku umbipka gusu, moshima no ku an.'

Orowa, nei shiwentep yupihi tura no nei tusu-guru kosakayokara. Awa, nei tusu-guru irushka wa ene itak-hi:—'Son no eani e shikashke hawe he an? Kuani anak ne, Kamui en turen gusu wen-buri e koro katu obitta ku eraman; awa, son no e irara gusu he e hawe an, sekoro itak. Orowa, son no e irara yakun, teeda anak ne wen-buri koro guru ene apakashnu-hi ne gusu, nei no echi pakashnu na.' Sekoro itak koro, hopuni wa 'shiwentep tekehe abe ku omare kusu ne,' sekoro itak. Orota, kuani anak ne shiwentep ishitomare hawe ne kuni ku ramu gusu, moshima no ku an. Awa, son no poka, shiwentep tekehe abe omare nisa ruwe ne. Orota kuani ene ku itak-hi:—'Shi no wen shiriki ne na;

A Case of Bewitching.

TRANSLATION—*continued*.

man prayed to God; nevertheless, the woman, denying the matter, went to the village of Nikap and fetched her husband; that young man said:—'Ask the medicine-man whether the woman really cut the clothes.' But as I did not believe she did it, I remained at home in bed. After this the elder brother of the woman called me to him, and he also said to me:—'Have your clothes not been cut because you are in love with some other woman?' I was very angry at this; and said, 'As for me, I am ill all the time and lying down, with what woman should I fall in love?' and 'as I thought it had been done by a little lad I took no notice of it, but this medicine-man says that the woman did it; however, as I disbelieved him I am allowing the matter to rest; but you have come to me and speak in this manner. As I do not believe it, I prefer to let the matter alone.'

After this the woman and her elder brother upbraided the medicine-man, whereupon he got angry and said: 'Do you indeed deny it? As for me, by the inspiration of God I know the whole of your evil deeds; and are you in truth so utterly depraved that you spoke so? Now as you behave in such a depraved manner I will punish you in the same way as was done in such cases in ancient time.' So saying he got up and said, 'I will put fire into the woman's hand.' Upon this, thinking that he said it to frighten her, I remained quiet. But he really did place fire in her hand. I then said to

THE AINU'S ACCOUNT—*continued.*

iteki nei no iki yan,' sekoro ku itak. Orowa, shinire ruwe ne; ainu obitta shini nisa ruwe ne.

Orowa, nei tusu-guru ene itak-hi :—' Son no shiwentep shikashke, shiwentep amip yaspa shimoki a yakun, tekehe shomo uhui nangoro gusu, ainu obitta shiruwande yan. Orowa, amip yaspa ishirishina wen-buri koro ayakun, tekehe uhui kem ki araka hem ki nangoro gusu, Ainu obitta shiruwande yan,' sekoro itak.

Orowa, kuani anak ne tusu-guru shi no wen-buri koro shiri ne kuni ku ramu koro, ku uni ta ku hoshipi wa ku an. Awa, nei a shiwentep tekehe uhui wa araka ruwe ne. Awa, nei tusu-guru ene itak-hi :—' Ingara yan, ene ani ne ; wen-buri koro yakun ene nehi ne na,' sekoro itak ruwe ne. Koroka, kuani anak ne shi no wen-buri ne kuni ku ramu gusu moshima no ku an. Awa, nei shiwentep yupihi tun-pish an ruwe ne ; awa, shine yupi shi no irushka hawe ene ani :—

'Nep gusu en sempirigeta echi en nure shomoki no shiwentep tekehe echi uhuika ya?' sekoro itak. Shi no irushka. Orota ene ku itak-hi :— 'Ku keutum shomo ne, tusu-guru keutum ne ; kuani anak ne shi no tusu-guru wen-buri koro shiri ne kuni ku ramu ruwe ne,' sekoro ku itak. Koroka nei guru shi no irushka wa ene itak-hi :— 'Nep gusu shomo echi en nure yakun, echi obitta echi keutem ne nangoro,' sekoro itak. Orowa, Yakusho nure nisa ruwe ne. Orowa, Yakusho orowa no kambi ek nisa. Tusu-guru hemhem, kuani hemhem, kugoro michi hemhem ahotuyekara kambi ek nisa ruwe ne. Orowa, tusu-

A Case of Bewitching.

Translation—*continued*.

them, 'Such a process is exceedingly bad, do not do it.' And I made them stop; all the people stopped.

Then the medicine man said, 'If the woman's denial is true, and she did not cut the clothes, her hand for that reason will not be burnt; let all the people watch. But if she did cut the clothes, and has wickedly bewitched the man, the hand will for that reason both burn and she suffer pain; let all the people watch.'

Now, as I thought that the medicine-man was acting in a very wicked way, I returned to my home. Then that woman's hand was burnt and she suffered pain. Upon this the medicine-man said: 'See here so it is; those who have done evil are affected so.' But as for me, considering the action to be very bad, I left them to themselves. Now, the woman had two elder brothers; and one of them being very angry spake thus:—

'Why have you secretly and without letting me know burnt the woman's hand?' He was very angry. I said to him: 'It was not my wish, but that of the medicine-man; as for me, I considered him to be acting very wickedly indeed.' But he, being exceedingly angry, said: 'If it be asked why you did not let me know, it was because you all took part in it.' He then reported the matter to the Japanese authorities. After this a summons came from the Government offices for the medicine-man, myself, and my father to appear in court. I went with the medicine-man, and we

The Ainu's Account—*continued.*

guru tura no ku oman ruwe ne. Yakusho otta ahup ash. Awa, 'nep gusu shiwentep tekehe uhuika ya' sekoro tono itak. Orota ene ku itak-hi:—'Kuani anak ne pon heikachi hene amip yaspa ruwe ne kuni ku ramu, awa, toan tusu-guru shiwentep ne sekoro itak koro tekehe abe omare nisa. Shi no wen shiri ne kuni ku ramu gusu iteki nei no iki yan sekoro ku itak ruwe ne, sekoro tono otta an korachi, shunge sak no ku ye nisa ruwe ne. Orowa, tono ene itak-hi:—'Nep gusu tan tusu-guru shiwentep tekehe e uhuika ya?' sekoro itak. Orowa tusu-guru ene itak-hi:—'Kuani anak ne Kamui en turen gusu, Kamui orowa no wen-buri nukan nisa. Tan shiwentep anak ne son no wen-buri koro ishirishina hem ki wa gusu, koro wen-buri obosore kusu ne; awa, koro yupo tura no ek wa ikosakayokara shikashke gusu wen no iye nisa wa gusu, Kamui irushka gusu, shiwentep apakashnu nisa ruwe ne,' sekoro itak. Orota tono ene itak-hi:—'Shi no wen-buri ne, shiwentep yupihi ne yakka shi no wen, nep gusu e utari-hi tekehe auhuika hike moshima no e an ya?' sekoro itak. Shi no nei guru aapapu ruwe ne. Orowa, 'tusu-guru anak ne nep Kamui turen wa tusu ya'? sekoro itak. Awa, upshoro wa chironnup sapa shinep, orowa chikap sapa shinep sange ruwe ne. Awa, tono utara shi no mina. 'Nep kamui ta okai ya? Ichakkere wen kamui ne gusu shitofu oshiketa omare wa uhuika kusu ne, sekoro tono utara itak. Awa, shi no tusu-guru ekimatek ruwe ne.

A Case of Bewitching.

TRANSLATION—*continued.*

entered the court together. After this the official said to me :—'Why have you burnt the woman's hand?' I replied saying :—'I thought that a little boy had cut my clothes, but that medicine-man there, saying that the woman cut them, placed some fire in her hand. Thinking that it was bad to do so, I told him to desist.' Indeed, I told him truly just as things happened. The official then said :—'Why did you—you medicine-man—burn the woman's hand?' The medicine-man said :—'As for me, it was because I was inspired by God, and because God had shown me her evil deeds. With reference to this woman it was because she acted so wickedly as to bewitch one, and because I was going to drive out the evil; but because she came with her elder brother and upbraided me, and because denying the fact she spoke against me, God was angry, and punished her.' The official said to them: 'This is a wicked thing. Both the woman and her brother are very bad, why did your relations leave you alone to have your hand burnt?' The man then begged for pardon. The official then said :—' Medicine-man, what gods inspired you to prophesy?' Thereupon he took out from his bosom the skulls of a fox and a bird. The officials laughed very heartily at this, and said :—'What gods are these? As they are filthy devils, we will burn them in the stove.' The medicine-man was very much frightened at this.

This is all there is in the case that I consider worth recording. That medicine-man was placed in prison for one night, and to his great joy and comfort allowed to take his fox and bird's skulls with him when he was released the next day. This is probably the very last case of bewitching and divination we shall ever hear of as taking place among this fast-disappearing people, and I consider myself fortunate to have had this one brought before me so fully. The man supposed to be bewitched is a Christian of two years' standing; this will account for his scepticism of the powers of the witch or medicine-man.

There are several things in this account well worth considering; and the first to which I would draw your attention is what the Ainu consider to be the nature of witchcraft.

1.—THE NATURE OF WITCHCRAFT.

The word *ishirishina*, which I have translated by the verb 'to bewitch,' really means in essence 'to bind up fast,' or 'to tie up tightly.' And thus with reference to the present psychological subject it comes to mean a binding up of the life, spirit or soul of a person. If it be asked with *what* the life, spirit, or soul be bound, the reply is, with *uoitakushi*, *i.e.* 'a cursing,' for this word is sometimes used as a synonym for 'to bewitch.' And if again it be asked by what process of words bewitching is accomplished, the reply is, by *Pion itak-ki*, *i.e.* 'doing the little talk,' which also means 'to mesmerize.' Again, should one ask what is the result of being

Nature of Witchcraft.

bewitched, the reply is in the present case, it is supposed to be a lingering illness ending in death. If it be asked how are the effects of the curse to be counteracted, the reply is, by the exorcism of the medicine-man. And if, lastly, one asks how the witch may be found out and made to confess, the answer is, call in the medicine-man to find out, and apply the ordeal of fire.

2.—The Use of the Fox and Bird's Skulls.

In the above account we were told that the Ainu, when asked by the Japanese officials as to what gods inspired him to know the culprit, he took from his bosom the skulls of a fox and bird. He had used these for divination; that was the part they played in the matter. I find among my papers a note on this very subject, which I take this opportunity of bringing into daylight. It is as follows:—

On some occasions when ordeal is not resorted to, a kind of divination is performed; but this is indulged in with the special purpose of finding out a culprit by the finger of the gods, and not through the confession of the supposed wicked doer himself. The following incident, which came under my direct observation, will well serve to illustrate my meaning.

In one of the Ainu villages in which I have spent many months, one of the men, with whom I am well acquainted, was one day very angry at having lost a paper dollar. He had a strong suspicion that a particular young woman, his daughter in fact, who was married and lived next door, had stolen the money. He accordingly accused her of the deed. But as she refused to confess, and stoutly and persistently denied the charge, her father proceeded to perform what the Ainu call by the various names of *niwok-ki marapto*, 'the ceremony of discovery;' *shitumbe marapto*, 'the ceremony of the fox;' or *kema koshne guru marapto*, 'the ceremony of the light-footed person,' the fox being so called on account of the rapidity with which it can get out of one's way.

This 'ceremony of the fox' is a sort of divination, by means of which the guilt or innocence of an accused person is supposed to be established, and is very closely allied to trial by ordeal. In the present case, however, though the person was brought in guilty, and implicit faith was placed in the decision, there appears to have been a mistake, for shortly afterwards the dollar was found; but it was quite against the father's dignity to tell his daughter so. I verily believe that he was angry to find out that his divination had played him false.

Every married Ainu keeps one fox's skull, carefully decorated with shavings, stowed away among his treasures in the eastern or sacred end of his hut. With this he divines, should he have lost anything, or should something have gone wrong in any other way with him. In such a case he takes the skull from its corner, and, after having prayed over it and told it all his troubles, asks it to make known to him the cause. Should the spirit

Divination.

of the skull be favourable it will show him the whole matter in a dream.

The ceremony concerning which I am now speaking was conducted as follows:—The accused person was brought into the hut of her father and made to sit in front of him. He then produced his fox's skull, prayed before it, told it of his loss, and asked it to favour him by answering truly. He next separated the lower jaw from the rest of the skull. The top part of the skull, which is called *sapa num*, was reverently put on one side, and the jaw placed upon his head, teeth upwards. He then gently lent forward so as to allow the jaw to gradually slip to the floor. As it fell with the teeth to the ground his daughter was thereby proved guilty; but should it have fallen with the teeth upwards she would have been declared innocent. The person proved guilty was called *ko-niwok guru*, 'the person pointed out' or 'discovered.'

Should it have happened, however, that the loser of the money had no suspicion as to the thief, he would have tied a long piece of string to the skull, and having gathered up the string in a bunch in his hand, would have caused an assembly of likely people each to take one piece of the string, and all pull together. He who took the piece immediately attached to the skull would have been the person pointed out as the culprit. It is needless to add that the Ainu have implicit confidence in this curious ceremony, though it does play them false sometimes. I should also remark that many Ainu men, when going on a long journey, reverently carry a fox's skull and a bird's head among their luggage;

with these they divine, and determine which way to take, or which of two things should be done next.

3.—External Methods of Bewitching.

In the case before us the clothes of the person supposed to be bewitched were found to have been cut with a pair of scissors. That is to say, a number of little holes were cut out of the garments. In the case of exorcism to which I have already directed the reader's attention, we found that the garments were cut with a sickle in long slits; these, we see, were cut with scissors and in little holes. The former was probably to kill an evil spirit outright for a good purpose, the present to kill a man slowly, out of spite or jealousy. There is some underlying mystery about this cutting which the Ainu cannot explain; the only reason they can give for it is that it is an old way of their forefathers, they therefore do it also.

Printed in the USA
CPSIA information can be obtained
at www.ICGtesting.com
LVHW042300280624
784232LV00002B/51

9 781528 772440